Advice from Your Challenging Emotions

Welcome to your personal field guide to the world of challenging emotions!

This book is divided into three parts: **Emotion Basics** to get you started, **Emotion Deep Dives** for a closer look at nine specific emotions, and **Next Steps** to take what you've learned forward. Whether you read it cover to cover or jump straight to an emotion that's puzzling you, this book is here to guide you. The details for each emotion offer insightful, actionable advice that turns challenging emotions from confusing reactions into opportunities for personal growth.

Ready to explore your emotions like never before? Let's do this!

Lisa C. Welsher

While every precaution has been taken in the preparation of this book, the publisher assumes no responsibility for errors or omissions, or for damages resulting from the use of the information contained in this book.

ADVICE FROM YOUR CHALLENGING EMOTIONS

First Edition. 1.0 August, 2024

Copyright © 2024 Lisa C. Welsher

Written by Lisa C. Welsher

Table of Contents

Introduction

In 1973, a music group called The Faces released a song called "Ooh La La." Written by Ronnie Lane and Ronnie Wood, this song features the famous line:

"I wish that I knew what I know now...
When I was younger."

The essence of the words lies in the universal experience of aging and gaining new perspectives that we often wish we had known earlier.

The song resonated with many listeners and has been recorded since by various artists, including Rod Stewart. The lyrics have also been featured in several different ad campaigns, helping to cement this phrase in popular culture.

When I hear the song, I think about emotions. When I was younger, I wish I had become more informed about emotions. This is because what I know now is that learning to work with my emotions rather than working against them has been an absolute game changer!

Contrary to popular belief, all emotions serve a purpose. Emotions are a part of who we are, and each one is designed to bring valuable information into our awareness—if, and that's a big if, we are willing to invest a little time learning about them.

This book is designed for educational purposes. It's intended to help you, the reader, become more informed about your emotions. It can serve as a starting point for anyone who is ready to build a solid foundation of Emotional Literacy, which is where it all begins!

Reflecting on the poignant lyrics of "Ooh La La," I'm reminded of the essence of hindsight and the value of the wisdom we gain over time. I'm glad you're here, and I'm glad you're ready to get started! Emotions shape the trajectory of our lives in profound ways. That's why I always think about emotions when I hear the lyrics *"I wish that I knew what I know now, when I was younger."*

Let's get started!

Emotion Basics

Part One: Emotion Basics

If you've ever rented a car, you're probably familiar with the last-minute stress of having to refuel before returning the vehicle. Working as a management consultant and routinely flying to different client locations, I was no stranger to car rentals and last-minute refueling. What made matters worse was that depending on the car model, sometimes the gas tank was on the left and other times it was on the right.

Inevitably, as I raced last-minute into a gas station, I'd usually pull up to the pump on the "wrong" side. This might seem like a minor inconvenience, having to reposition the car so the gas tank was on the correct side, but when you're racing against the clock to catch a flight, every minute matters.

Then one day, I found myself sitting at a bar in an airport, waiting for a delayed flight. I was exchanging stories with a fellow traveler when they mentioned, "So, I guess you don't know there's a tiny triangle next to the fuel icon in every car. The location of the triangle indicates which side the fuel tank is on."

There it was. My "aha" moment that would change rental car refueling from that day forward!

There are four key concepts included in Part One of this book. You may experience them as "aha" moments or, alternatively, you may resist them. People have a lot of preconceived notions about emotions. Unfortunately, many of these notions are incorrect.

As you read through the content in Part One, I invite you to keep an open mind. Consider donning your scientist's lab coat and engaging with curiosity, rather than wearing your Judge Judy robe. The foundation of knowledge established in Part One sets the stage for Part Two, which includes a deep dive into nine challenging emotions.

Let's take the first step!

The Human Experience: Embracing Life's Full Spectrum

Americans spend about 20,000 hours in formal education, yet receive little to no instruction on understanding emotions. This educational gap persists into higher education, where an additional 5,000 to 6,000 hours dedicated to obtaining a four-year degree still rarely touch on navigating our emotional landscapes.

This lack of emotional education is significant, considering that the human experience is deeply intertwined with a broad spectrum of emotions. For instance, encountering a grizzly bear might trigger fear, while the birth of a child might elicit joy. Loss might plunge us into grief, just as receiving an award might elevate us into happiness.

The human experience is rich with both challenging emotions like anger, grief, sadness, or shame, and more pleasant emotions like happiness, excitement, and joy. Central to understanding this experience is recognizing the natural balance of emotions we encounter. Life's inherent ebb and flow bring about a mix of experiences, leading to a varied emotional landscape. This constant flux of events and corresponding emotions encapsulates the essence of life.

Chasing after perpetual happiness is an unrealistic expectation that ignores the inherent nature of human existence. Life's ups and downs mean that we will inevitably face periods of difficulty alongside moments of joy. Accepting the full range of human emotions as normal and valuable, rather than constantly striving for an unattainable ideal of constant happiness, fosters resilience and a healthier, more empowered approach to navigating life's complexities.

The pursuit of constant happiness is unrealistic because the human experience inherently includes both highs and lows. Recognizing and embracing the full spectrum of emotions as normal and valuable is essential for developing resilience and a healthier approach to life's complexities.

This is why the ability to accept the full range of emotions begins with busting a long-standing myth that emotions are either positive or negative. This simply isn't true.

No Negative Emotions:
All Emotions Welcome

In the era before digital communication, messengers on horseback delivered news across battlefields and kingdoms. These individuals often bore the brunt of negative reactions if the news was unfavorable, blamed not for their message's content but merely for its delivery. This historical scenario mirrors how we sometimes treat our emotions, especially when they're challenging or uncomfortable. Rather than "shooting the messenger," we should be tuning in to the invaluable insights that these emotions are attempting to convey.

Western culture tends to dichotomize emotions as "negative" or "positive." Yet, labeling an emotion as "negative" just because it feels uncomfortable overlooks its inherent value. Every emotion, from the anxiety that challenges our coping mechanisms to the joy that enhances our well-being, carries important information about the way we interpret the world around us, our experiences and ourselves.

It's essential to recognize that emotions themselves are neither negative nor positive; rather, it is the thinking that precedes emotions or our response to these emotions that colors our perceptions. By becoming more informed about emotions and adjusting our thinking and our reactions, we can reshape our understanding and appreciation of all emotions.

Consider a fresh perspective on emotions: they are not obstacles in our path, but rather guides along our journey. Just as a compass offers direction, emotions provide insights that help us navigate the complexities of life.

Rethinking our approach to emotions allows us to see them not as hindrances but as trusted advisors, providing valuable guidance through life's ups and downs.

Trusted Advisors:
Emotions as Guides to Insight

Picture the dynamic between a golf professional and their caddy during a round. This relationship isn't just about carrying clubs; it's a strategic partnership where the caddy assesses distances, evaluates conditions, recommends clubs, and supports the golfer's decisions. The caddy is a trusted advisor whose insights can significantly impact the game.

Similarly, our emotions are like caddies for our psyche, each bringing unique information and insights to our consciousness. Just as our bodies have various parts like bones, muscles, and organs, each with specific functions, our emotional spectrum includes a range of emotions, each serving a distinct and valuable role in our lives.

By learning to trust and understand the messages our emotions convey, we begin to work with them, not against them. This shift in approach transforms how we handle life's challenges and our interactions with others, leading to more effective and improved outcomes and results. Embracing our emotions as trusted advisors paves the way for deeper self-awareness and intuitive decision-making, empowering us to navigate life with greater ease and effectiveness.

Think of emotions not as mere disturbances or random feelings, but as guides—trusted advisors designed to offer us unique insights and valuable information, it opens up a whole new world of opportunity. However, it's not just about embracing emotions. Emotions are designed to come and go.

Ebb and flow. Activate and deactivate. When they are active,
they are looking for us to take a suitable action.

Emotions as a Call to Action: Indicator Lights of the Soul

Think of the array of light indicators on a modern car's dashboard. Each light serves as an alert to maintain the car in optimal condition, guiding actions that ensure the vehicle's longevity and safety. For example, the fuel light suggests it's time to refuel, and the tire pressure light indicates a need to check and adjust tire air levels. Similarly, alerts for low windshield wiper fluid or engine issues prompt immediate actions to prevent potential problems.

This is much how our emotions function. Triggered by our thoughts and perceptions, emotions act as indicators, prompting us to take specific actions. Addressing the need highlighted by an emotion, much like responding to a car's alert, resolves the issue and diminishes the emotion's intensity. Emotions are designed to be transient; they ebb and flow, activate and deactivate, signaling a need, and once that need is met through suitable action, they recede.

Understanding emotions as calls to action empowers us to respond to our inner signals with awareness and purpose. By recognizing and addressing the needs our emotions indicate, we are empowered to navigate our emotional landscape more effectively, supporting conflict resolution, healthy relationships, and personal growth. This perspective transforms our view of emotional experiences from being mere obstacles to navigational aids on our life journey.

Emotions serve as crucial signals, akin to a car's dashboard indicator lights. They guide us to take appropriate action in response to our needs, helping us navigate our emotional well-being with awareness and intention.

This may all sound straightforward, but it can be tricky. This is because when an emotion is active, our responses can fall into one of three categories. The chosen response directly impacts our outcomes and results for better or for worse.

3 Responses to Emotions: React, Repress, or Engage

Imagine you're on the game show "Let's Make a Deal," faced with choosing between three mystery doors, each hiding a different outcome. This scenario mirrors the three fundamental responses we have to emotions: reacting, repressing, and engaging. The choice you make significantly influences your outcomes and results.

- **Reacting:** This is the instinctive, immediate response. For instance, in anger, you might lash out or blame others. This reaction often overlooks the deeper messages your emotions are trying to convey, acting hastily without considering the underlying causes or consequences.

- **Repressing:** Repressing an emotion involves attempts to push it out of your conscious awareness, often because it's overwhelming or you are concerned about others' reactions. While this might offer temporary relief, it prevents you from accessing the insights and resolutions that come with engaging with your emotions.

- **Engaging:** This approach requires cultivation through emotional literacy and intelligence. It involves a thoughtful investigation into the root causes of an emotion, followed by deliberate action. Engaging with emotions means choosing to work constructively with them, recognizing their value as catalysts for self-awareness and growth, rather than working against them.

Choosing how to respond to our emotions is akin to selecting the right door on "Let's Make a Deal." While reacting and repressing may seem easier in the short term, they often lead to less favorable outcomes. Understanding the three basic responses to emotions—reacting, repressing, and engaging—is very important. Opting to engage constructively with our emotions minimizes unnecessary drama and needless suffering which leads to an improved ability to navigate life's ups and downs.

But before you can engage with emotions, you need to understand the purpose of each emotion. Let's do this! Let's take a deep dive into 9 challenging emotions that once understood, can radically change the way you respond to them!

Emotion Deep Dives

STAGES OF
LEARNING

Part Two: Emotion Deep Dives

Before you read about each of the emotion deep dives, I'd like to shed a little light on two important concepts that could hinder your ability to fully understand what you're about to read.

The first is called the Four Stages of Competence. This concept is widely attributed to Noel Burch and was popularized in the 1970s. The four stages can be summarized as follows:
1. **Unconscious Incompetence**: Not knowing what you don't know.
2. **Conscious Incompetence**: Realizing what you don't know.
3. **Conscious Competence**: Knowing how to do something but needing to concentrate on it.
4. **Unconscious Competence**: Performing a skill effortlessly without conscious thought.

These are the basic four steps that capture the progression of learning something new and developing the associated skills.

When it comes to emotions, I dare say a lot of people (it might even be safe to say most people) are in stage one—they don't know what they don't know. My intention in writing this book is to help readers unlock the door to a whole new way of looking at emotions. The goal, first and foremost, is to help you realize what you don't know about emotions. I've also tried to pave the way for you to learn a bit about how to work with your emotions!

The key is to keep an open mind. When you're in stage one and don't know what you don't know, it can be easy to miss out on a lot of valuable insights.

The second concept is "Cognitive Interference" or "Interference Theory." This psychological theory explains how previously learned information can obstruct the learning of new material. It often complicates the learning process because it involves unlearning or modifying what was previously understood.

Taking advice from your challenging emotions can be a tough pill to swallow, especially considering all the preconceived notions you may have about constantly striving for happiness and avoiding "negative" emotions at all costs.

The process of becoming more informed about your emotions will likely involve some cognitive interference, as your existing knowledge about emotions may obstruct your understanding of these new concepts.

As with Part One, I strongly encourage you to engage with an open mind. Understanding that all emotions serve a purpose—as messengers bringing valuable information to your awareness—can be transformative. You can discover a dormant superpower within you but expect some interference as you work to replace old habits and outdated thinking with new, empowering knowledge and skills!

Okay! That's enough. Let's kick things off with Anger!

Think of anger
not just as a
signal of what's
wrong, but also,
as an invitation
to set things
right.

Meet Your Anger

Think of anger as a proactive friend. It steps up to inform you when something happens that doesn't sit well with your values or beliefs. Engaging with anger is not just about feeling upset; it's about using that feeling to connect better with others through effective communication and by setting healthy boundaries.

Detailed Explanation of Anger

Anger is often seen through a negative lens, but in reality, it's an essential part of our emotional toolkit. This emotion springs into action when our values and beliefs are challenged, whether by someone's actions or by situations that cross our moral boundaries. Anger has a constructive role: it communicates to us—and motivates us to communicate to others—what we stand for and what we won't stand for.

When you express your anger effectively, it opens a channel for deeper understanding and connection. By effectively articulating why you're angry, you invite others into your personal world, sharing with them what matters to you. This doesn't just clear the air; it deepens bonds. People get to know the real you—your principles, your boundaries, and your cares. In this way, anger, when you engage with it constructively, can actually foster a sense of belonging and community. It tells others that you trust them enough to show your true feelings and that you value the relationship enough to work through conflicts.

Thus, engaging with anger is not about unleashing it on others, but about using it as a tool for mutual understanding and respect. It encourages not only personal integrity but also collective cohesion, guiding us towards interactions that are deeply aligned with our values and beliefs.

Advice from Anger

If anger could give you some friendly advice, it would likely say:

- *"Channel me constructively to assert your needs and set clear boundaries, transforming me into a tool for positive change and advocacy."*

- *"Engage with me by focusing on your actions, not by trying to control others."*

- *"Use me as a guide to uncover what truly matters to you, shedding light on any values and beliefs that may be compromised."*

"Use me as a guide to uncover what truly matters to you, shedding light on any values and beliefs that may be compromised."
ANGER

Mood-State Anger

Emotions are meant to be transient. They should arise when needed and settle after their job is done. If not addressed, anger can linger, becoming a mood with symptoms like:

- **Chronic Irritability:** Small annoyances might easily upset you, a sign of unresolved anger.

- **Hostility:** A lasting sense of antagonism can sour interactions and impact relationships negatively.

- **Aggression:** An increase in verbal or physical aggression can be a sign of anger that is going unresolved.

Coping Skills for Anger

All emotions arise with varying levels of intensity. When navigating intense anger, these skills can empower you to engage more effectively:

- **Deep Breathing:** Slow, deep breathing can calm your nervous system and lessen the intensity of your anger.

- **Physical Exercise:** Physical activity can channel anger constructively, releasing tension and boosting your mood with endorphins.

- **Time-Outs:** Stepping away from a situation that stirs up anger can give you space to cool down and think more clearly about your response.

Repressing, Reacting, & Engaging with Anger

Your response to anger can significantly shape your experiences. Suppose a valued friend keeps canceling on you last minute and it bothers you...

Repress	**React**	**Engage**
Ignoring your irritation and pretending it's okay is repressing anger.	Losing your temper or abruptly ending the friendship over cancellations is reacting in the heat of anger.	A better approach? Discuss your feelings with your friend, explain the impact of their actions, and explore ways to make plans more reliable.

Positive Outcomes of Engaging with Your Anger:

- **Improved Assertiveness:** Using anger constructively can boost your assertiveness, helping you set clear boundaries and stand up for your needs.

- **Conflict Resolution:** Getting to the heart of why you're angry can lead to effective problem-solving, which can improve your interactions and relationships.

- **Personal Growth:** Understanding what triggers your anger provides valuable insights into your values and beliefs, fostering personal development.

Ideas for Supporting Someone Else's Anger

Emotionally Intelligent Options	Not so Emotionally Intelligent Options
"Seems like you might be upset. Would you like to talk about what's bothering you?"	*"You're overreacting. Just calm down."*
"It's okay to feel angry. I'm here if you need someone to listen."	Laughing off their concerns or dismissing their anger as if they are trivial.
Offer a calm presence, giving them space to express themselves without judgment.	Ignoring them completely, or changing the subject abruptly to avoid discussing what made them angry.

Guilt isn't about self-punishment. It's about fine-tuning our actions to match our aspirations and desired outcomes.

GUILT

Meet Your Guilt

Guilt serves as an internal alert when there's a mismatch between our actions and our beliefs. It encourages us to pause and reflect whether our actions are in line with our moral values. This emotional signal is essential for maintaining integrity, helping us prevent regrettable actions or correct past missteps. Unlike shame, which arises when you're doubting your overall self-worth, guilt arises in response to a specific behavior.

Detailed Explanation of Guilt

Guilt is an introspective emotion that surfaces when our actions do not align with our principles. It not only prompts self-reflection; it also compels us to avoid future missteps and to make amends for past ones. Openly addressing our guilt can lead to stronger connections with others. By sharing our regrets and how we plan to address them, we invite others to understand our true values, enhancing mutual understanding and connection.

Advice from Guilt

If guilt could give you some friendly advice, it would likely say:

- *"See me as a reminder to review and realign your actions with your core values and beliefs, aiding in personal and ethical development."*

- *"Remember to separate me from shame—I focus on specific actions rather than your self-worth to foster constructive change and personal betterment."*

- *"Let me motivate you to rectify wrongs, turning lapses into chances for improvement and relationship building."*

Mood-State Guilt

Emotions are designed to be ephemeral, prompting needed actions and subsiding afterwards. If unresolved, guilt can linger and evolve into a mood state, with symptoms like:

- **Perpetual Self-Blame:** Constantly feeling at fault for negative outcomes, regardless of your direct involvement.

- **Low Self-Esteem:** Ongoing guilt can eventually add up, eroding your sense of self-worth.

- **Avoidance Behaviors:** Avoiding people or situations related to guilt can lead to unresolved conflicts and isolation.

"Let me motivate you to rectify wrongs, turning lapses into chances for improvement and relationship building."
GUILT

Coping Skills for Guilt

All emotions arise with varying levels of intensity. When navigating intense guilt, these skills can empower you to engage more effectively:

- **Self-Compassion Exercises:** Practice self-kindness, addressing yourself as you would a friend in the same situation.

- **Behavior-Focused Reflection:** Write about your actions that led to feelings of guilt to explore their misalignment with your values.

- **Seeking Feedback:** Consult a trusted friend or relative about your feelings to gain a clearer, more objective perspective.

Repressing, Reacting, & Engaging with Guilt

Your response to guilt can significantly shape your experiences. Let's say you catch yourself gossiping about someone and regret the things you've said...

Repress	React	Engage
Ignoring feelings of guilt after engaging in gossip and acting like nothing happened.	Over-apologizing without fully understanding the impact or avoiding the aggrieved person.	Acknowledging the error, sincerely apologizing to those impacted, and implementing measures to prevent recurrence.

Positive Outcomes of Engaging with Guilt:

- **Restorative Actions:** Taking steps to correct mistakes or mend fences not only improves relationships but also reinforces our ethical commitments.

- **Enhanced Self-awareness:** Understanding what prompts our guilt increases our awareness of our values and motivates us to align our actions accordingly.

- **Self-Discipline:** Addressing guilt head-on can strengthen our resolve to act ethically, improving our overall outcomes and personal development.

Ideas for Supporting Someone Else's Guilt

Emotionally Intelligent Options	Not so Emotionally Intelligent Options
"It sounds like you're disappointed in something you did. Want to share what happened?"	*"You should feel guilty; what you did was terrible."*
"We all make mistakes. What will you do differently next time?"	Telling them they're always messing things up without offering any constructive feedback.
Help them explore ways to make amends or to forgive themselves, reinforcing their capacity for growth.	Minimizing their feelings by comparing them to more significant problems or telling them to just get over it.

Envy can
actually serve
as a roadmap to
our deepest
desires and
aspirations.

Meet Your Envy

Envy is the emotion that arises when we notice discrepancies in the allocation of rewards, resources, or recognition compared to others. This emotion can alert us to what we may feel is lacking in our lives and prompts us to consider whether these perceived inequities are due to our own actions or external factors. Engaging with envy provides an opportunity to either adjust our own behaviors to better align with our goals or to advocate for ourselves when we believe we deserve more.

Detailed Explanation of Envy

Often seen in a negative light, envy is actually a powerful indicator of where we perceive inequalities in our life, especially concerning recognition, rewards, and resources. It stems from wanting something we don't have that someone else has, highlighting areas where we feel fairness may be absent. By constructively engaging with envy, we can uncover these perceived injustices and either make personal changes or seek to correct external disparities. This process not only aids in personal development but also promotes a more equitable distribution of opportunities and resources.

Advice from Envy

If envy could give you some friendly advice, it would likely say:

- *"Observe where you feel a lack and what you desire more of—be it resources, recognition, or opportunities—and reassess your goals accordingly."*

- *"After carefully assessing a situation, if you still believe you are deserving, advocate for yourself."*

- *"Harness my energy for your growth, both personal and professional, by identifying and addressing the gaps between where you are and where you want to be."*

Mood-State Envy

Emotions are meant to be transient, prompting us to take action and then dissipating. However, when envy is not effectively addressed, it can solidify into a persistent mood state characterized by:

- **Resentment:** A lasting bitterness towards others' successes or possessions.

- **Dissatisfaction:** An ongoing dissatisfaction with one's own achievements.

- **Social Withdrawal:** Withdrawing from social interactions to avoid the discomfort of envy, potentially leading to isolation.

"Harness my energy for your growth, both personal and professional, by identifying and addressing the gaps between where you are and where you want to be."

ENVY

Coping Skills for Envy

All emotions arise with varying levels of intensity. When navigating intense envy, these skills can empower you to engage more effectively:

- **Gratitude Journaling:** Focus on what you are grateful for in your life, which can shift attention away from what you perceive as missing.

- **Minimize Social Media:** Consider stepping away from social media; it is a breeding ground for envy.

- **Setting Personal Goals:** Direct your energy towards personal achievements by setting clear, actionable goals for yourself, shifting focus from envy to personal advancement.

Repressing, Reacting, & Engaging with Envy

Your response to envy can significantly influence your personal and professional outcomes. Let's say a peer at work receives a promotion you were hoping for...

Repress	React	Engage
Ignoring envy when a peer receives a promotion you aspired to, pretending it doesn't affect you.	Criticizing the colleague's achievements or withdrawing from team efforts.	Reflecting on what the promotion meant to you and seeking feedback to better understand the decision-making process to improve your own prospects.

- **Clarity on Desires:** Envy can highlight what is truly important to us, clarifying our desires and values.

- **Motivation for Self-improvement:** By acknowledging and understanding our envy, we can use it as a catalyst for personal development and moving closer to our goals.

- **Self-Advocacy:** Engaging with envy helps develop the ability to self-advocate for the rewards, resources, and recognition for which you feel you are genuinely entitled.

Ideas for Supporting Someone Else's Envy

Emotionally Intelligent Options	Not so Emotionally Intelligent Options
"Is there something someone else has that you want or think you deserve?"	*"Why can't you just be happy for them?"*
"It's natural to feel envious sometimes. What is it that you desire?"	Accusing them of being petty or envious without understanding their feelings.
Encourage them to identify and pursue their own goals and aspirations, emphasizing their unique path.	Boasting about your own achievements or happiness in areas they feel lacking, without consideration for their situation.

Fear is like a guardian, alerting us to potential real-time dangers that require our immediate attention and care.

Meet Your Fear

Fear is an intuitive alert that arises in response to real or perceived threats to our physical or emotional safety. This emotion can also extend to protecting those we care about. Engaging with fear allows us to either avoid a threat or prepare to face it, supporting our safety and the safety of others.

Detailed Explanation of Fear

Fear is our body's natural response to danger. It serves as a vital warning system, alerting us to threats that could harm us physically or emotionally. This emotion is rooted in the present, reacting to immediate risks. By paying attention to fear, we can create strategies to reduce or manage these threats effectively, helping us to protect ourselves and our loved ones.

Although fear and anxiety are similar emotions, fear arises in response to real-time, current threats while anxiety arises in response to future threats.

Advice from Fear

If fear could give you some friendly advice, it would likely say:
- *"Evaluate the legitimacy of the signals I send you, differentiating between baseless worries and genuine threats to navigate safely."*

- *"Use my presence as a motivation for taking action, not as an obstacle to living your life fully and pursuing personal growth."*

- *"Listen to me as your personal alert system for both real and perceived dangers, guiding your protective actions."*

Mood-State Fear

Emotions are meant to be transient, prompting necessary actions and resolving once those actions are taken. If fear is not adequately addressed, it can develop into a chronic mood state, with symptoms like:
- **Unease:** A constant feeling of fear, even in safe situations.

- **Avoidance:** Regularly avoiding circumstances or people that provoke fear, which can restrict personal growth and experiences.

- **Hypervigilance:** An excessive readiness to perceive threats, which can be draining and cause undue stress.

"Listen to me as your personal alert system for both real and perceived dangers, guiding your protective actions."
FEAR

Coping Skills for Fear

All emotions arise with varying levels of intensity. When navigating intense fear, these skills can empower you to engage more effectively:

- **Progressive Muscle Relaxation:** Tense and then slowly relax each muscle group, which can help alleviate the physical symptoms of fear.

- **Visualization:** Picture yourself handling the feared situation successfully, which can boost your confidence.

- **Information Gathering:** Educate yourself about the source of your fear. Understanding the facts can often reduce the intensity of fear, leading to more rational responses.

Repressing, Reacting, & Engaging with Fear

Your response to fear can significantly influence your physical and emotional safety. Let's say you're in a store and a smoke alarm goes off...

Repress	React	Engage
Ignoring the smoke alarm and continuing to shop.	Panicking and running immediately when the alarm sounds, without assessing the situation.	Pausing to quickly assess the situation when the alarm sounds, then deciding on the best course of action based on the information available.

Positive Outcomes When You Engage with Fear:

- **Enhanced Decision-making:** Recognizing and evaluating your fear allows you to make clearer, more informed decisions about real and imagined risks.

- **Personal Safety:** By listening to fear, you can avoid real dangers, using it as a safeguard.

- **Courage Development:** Confronting and overcoming fears can build courage, enhancing your ability to handle future challenges.

Ideas for Supporting Someone Else's Fear

Emotionally Intelligent Options	Not so Emotionally Intelligent Options
"Do you want to talk about what's frightening you?"	*"That's irrational; there's nothing to be afraid of."*
"I'm willing to just listen if you want to talk about what you think is threatening your physical or emotional safety."	Mocking their fears or daring them to face them without thinking objectively and/or providing support or understanding.
Offer reassurance and, if appropriate, help them develop a plan to address their fears.	Dismissing their concerns and insisting they confront their fear without consideration for the root cause.

Anxiety is a frequently misunderstood attempt at preparing us for future challenges, asking us to plan rather than panic.

ANXIETY

Meet Your Anxiety

Anxiety is an emotion that signals a potential future threat to our physical or emotional well-being, or that of someone important to us, especially when we feel unprepared or pessimistic. Engaging with anxiety gives us a chance to plan and execute tasks that increase our preparedness.

Detailed Explanation of Anxiety

Anxiety takes the concept of fear and projects it into the future, marked by feelings of unpreparedness and foreboding about upcoming challenges. This emotion acts as a spur for planning and preparation, turning worry into actionable strategies. By proactively addressing anxiety, we can improve our readiness, moving from doubt to a state of enhanced preparedness and confidence.

Advice from Anxiety

If anxiety could give you some friendly advice, it would likely say:

- *"Focus on what you can control and let go of what you cannot, directing your efforts towards actionable solutions."*

- *"Leverage me to develop resilience and coping strategies, turning potential stress into a clear plan for action."*

- *"See me as a reflection of your deep care and concern for the future. Use this energy for productive planning and preparation."*

Mood-State Anxiety

Emotions are meant to be transient, designed to prompt specific actions and then subside. However, if anxiety is not addressed with appropriate actions, it can solidify into a mood state, characterized by:

- **Generalized Anxiety:** Ongoing worries about a wide array of issues, irrespective of their actual probability or impact.

- **Restlessness:** A persistent feeling of being 'on edge', making it hard to relax.

- **Sleep Disturbances:** Trouble falling or staying asleep, often due to relentless negative thoughts.

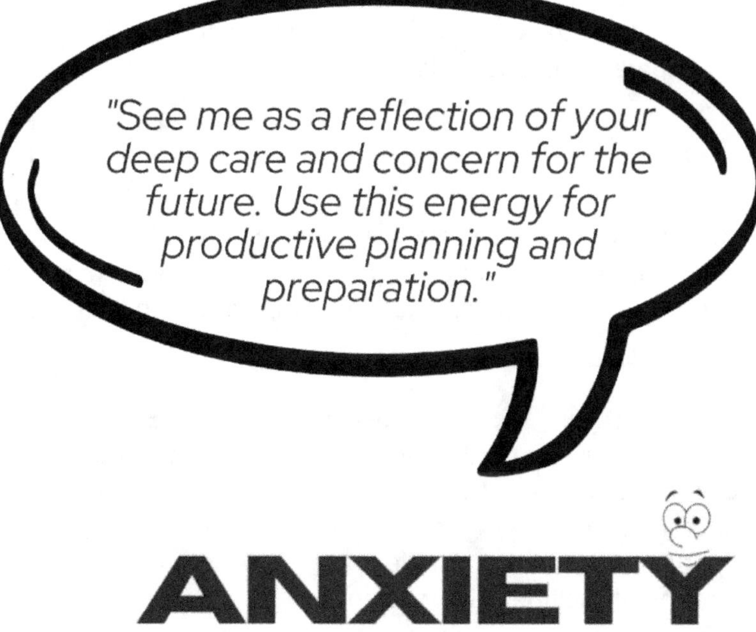

"See me as a reflection of your deep care and concern for the future. Use this energy for productive planning and preparation."
ANXIETY

Coping Skills for Anxiety

All emotions arise with varying levels of intensity. When navigating intense anxiety, these skills can empower you to engage more effectively:

- **Breathing Techniques:** Practice calming breathing exercises, such as the 4-7-8 technique, to reduce anxiety.

- **Mindfulness and Meditation:** Engage in mindfulness exercises to focus on the present, minimizing worries about the future.

- **Directed Thinking:** Concentrate your thoughts on proactive measures you are taking to become more prepared and less anxious.

Repressing, Reacting, & Engaging with Anxiety

Your response to anxiety can significantly influence your physical and emotional safety. Let's say you have an upcoming interview for a job you want but aren't prepared for...

Repress	React	Engage
Ignoring persistent worries about the approaching interview, acting as if everything is fine.	Becoming obsessed with the interview details to the point of losing sleep and being unable to focus on actual preparation.	Acknowledging your anxiety, researching common interview questions, practicing responses, and seeking feedback to enhance your readiness and confidence.

Positive Outcomes When You Engage with Anxiety:

- **Preparedness:** Anxiety can drive you to thoroughly prepare for anticipated events, improving performance and reducing uncertainty.

- **Problem-solving Skills:** Confronting the sources of your anxiety helps you develop robust problem-solving skills, allowing you to tackle the underlying issues effectively.

- **Time Management:** By understanding your anxiety, you can enhance your time management skills, prioritizing efforts that increase preparedness.

Ideas for Supporting Someone Else's Anxiety

Emotionally Intelligent Options	Not so Emotionally Intelligent Options
- *"Is there something you're worried about?*	- *"Just stop worrying so much; it's not that big of a deal."*
- *"Can I help you work through the steps you can take to get better prepared?"*	- Telling them they're always anxious about something and need to chill.
- Provide a listening ear, allowing them to organize their thoughts and concerns.	- Ignoring their requests for support or reassurance because you think their anxiety is an overreaction.

Jealousy ultimately reveals the relationships we value and the connections we fear to lose.

Meet Your Jealousy

Jealousy is an emotion that alerts you to threats—real or perceived—that might affect a significant relationship. Whether it's a bond with a loved one, like a spouse or sibling, or with someone influential like a boss or teacher, jealousy serves as a signal that a valued relationship is potentially at risk.

Detailed Explanation of Jealousy

Jealousy acts as a guardian for the relationships we have and value, sounding the alarm when these important bonds might be at risk. Unlike envy, which arises from wanting something we don't have that someone else has—like their achievements or material gains—jealousy springs from the fear of losing an important connection. It encourages us to nurture and protect our relationships with loved ones or key figures in our lives. By positively addressing jealousy, we can solidify our bonds, making sure they're healthy and strong enough to withstand any potential disturbances. This proactive approach helps us to preserve and enhance the relationships that mean the most to us.

Advice from Jealousy

If jealousy could give you some friendly advice, it would likely say:

- *"Recognize me as a cue to scrutinize the dynamics of your relationships, helping you differentiate between real issues and mere suspicions."*

- *"Reflect on why I have emerged, consider any personal insecurities you might need to address, and use this insight to fortify your relationships."*

- *"Use this moment to engage in open communication with those you care about, which can lead to greater honesty and understanding."*

Mood-State Jealousy

Emotions are intended to be temporary, sparking necessary actions and then subsiding. When jealousy isn't properly managed, it can evolve into a chronic state with symptoms like:

- **Insecurity:** Persistent doubts about your worth or the stability of your relationships.

- **Trust Issues:** Continued challenges in trusting others, which can hinder the formation of healthy bonds.

- **Obsessive Thoughts:** Constant rumination over the subjects of your jealousy, disrupting normal life activities.

"Use this moment to engage in open communication with those you care about, which can lead to greater honesty and understanding."

JEALOUSY

Coping Skills for Jealousy

All emotions arise with varying levels of intensity. When navigating intense jealousy, these skills can empower you to engage more effectively:

- **Self-reflection:** Evaluate the reasons behind your jealousy and any underlying insecurities contributing to these feelings.

- **Communication:** Constructively express your concerns to those involved, fostering understanding and possibly resolving tensions.

- **Self-esteem Building Activities:** Participate in activities that reinforce your self-worth and confidence.

Repressing, Reacting, & Engaging with Jealousy

Your response to jealousy can significantly influence the security of relationships that are important to you. Let's say you feel like your lifetime best friend is no longer prioritizing your friendship...

Repress	**React**	**Engage**
Ignoring your discomfort when your friend starts spending more time with someone new, while internally feeling excluded and upset.	Accusing your friend of neglect or emotionally pulling away from the relationship out of hurt.	Discussing your feelings with your friend, expressing the importance of your relationship, and exploring ways to adjust to the new dynamics.

- **Relationship Enhancement:** Directly addressing feelings of jealousy can lead to better communication and stronger, more secure relationships.

- **Self-esteem Improvement:** Exploring the underlying causes of jealousy can help identify personal growth areas, enhancing self-esteem.

- **Value Clarification:** Reflecting on jealousy helps clarify what you truly value in relationships, guiding more authentic life choices.

Ideas for Supporting Someone Else's Jealousy

Emotionally Intelligent Options	Not so Emotionally Intelligent Options
"I sense some tension. Is there something you're feeling uneasy about?"	*"You're just jealous because I'm spending time with someone else."*
"It's natural to feel jealous sometimes. Why do you feel the relationship is at risk?"	Making them feel guilty for experiencing jealousy, rather than addressing the underlying concerns.
Encourage open communication about their feelings and reassure them of their value in the relationship.	Flaunting the stability of your own relationships.

Sadness offers us a profound opportunity to pause, reflect, release, and ultimately find a new path forward.

SADNESS

Meet Your Sadness

Sadness is the emotion that signals when you're dealing with unmet expectations that cause you pain. It prompts you to evaluate your expectations, release what's not working, and make space for new experiences and opportunities. Engaging with sadness allows you to pinpoint what's not working in your life and release it, paving the way for a fresh start and new pursuits.

Detailed Explanation of Sadness

Sadness arises when we face unmet expectations that bring about pain, prompting a need for reflection and release. This emotion serves as a profound signal, highlighting areas in our lives where adjustments and healing might be necessary. Whether sadness emerges directly from disappointment or follows feelings like anger or frustration, it always invites us to pause and re-evaluate our circumstances.

By engaging with sadness, we embark on a healing process that involves acknowledging our losses and letting go of what no longer benefits us. This opens up space in our hearts and minds for new experiences and opportunities. Sadness, therefore, not only helps us process past pains and disappointments but also prepares us for future growth, ensuring that we are more aligned with our true desires and needs as we move forward.

Advice from Sadness

If sadness could give you some friendly advice, it would likely say:

- *"Use me to help you identify what's missing or unfulfilled in your life and inspire you to seek new joys and contentment."*

- *"Share your feelings with trusted friends or family. Expressing and acknowledging your sadness can lighten your emotional load, strengthen your connections, and facilitate meaningful changes."*

- *"Allow yourself to recognize and accept unmet expectations and then release what's no longer working."*

Mood-State Sadness

Emotions are intended to be transient, activating to encourage a specific action and deactivating once that action is taken. However, if sadness isn't appropriately addressed, it can evolve into a persistent mood state, characterized by:

- **Depression:** Extended periods of low mood and a disinterest in activities once enjoyed.

- **Withdrawal:** Pulling back from social interactions and relationships.

- **Fatigue:** Ongoing tiredness or energy loss not caused by physical activity.

"Allow yourself to recognize and accept unmet expectations and then release what's no longer working."

SADNESS

Coping Skills for Sadness

All emotions arise with varying levels of intensity. When navigating intense sadness, these skills can empower you to engage more effectively:

- **Creative Expression:** Channel your emotions into art, music, writing, or other creative activities to process your feelings.

- **Physical Activity:** Physical exercise or spending time outdoors can boost your mood and energy levels.

- **Social Support:** Connect with friends or family for support or to discuss your feelings, which can help lighten your emotional load.

Repressing, Reacting, & Engaging with Sadness

Your response to sadness can significantly influence your outcomes and results. Let's say you wish your adult child would come to visit more often...

Repress	React	Engage
Ignoring your feelings of disappointment and maintaining a cheerful facade.	Demanding that your child needs to visit you more often because it's selfish of them not to!	Allowing yourself to feel and express the disappointment then actively seeking ways to release the unmet expectations so you can move forward with a "new normal."

Positive Outcomes When You Engage with Sadness:

- **Emotional Release:** Allowing yourself to fully experience sadness can lead to a cathartic release, clearing emotional blockages and facilitating healing.

- **Increased Compassion:** Understanding your own sadness can deepen your empathy and sensitivity towards others' struggles.

- **Depth of Experience:** Acknowledging and accepting sadness enriches your emotional life, enhancing your appreciation for both the highs and lows.

Ideas for Supporting Someone Else's Sadness

Emotionally Intelligent Options	Not so Emotionally Intelligent Options
"It seems like you're hurting. I'm here if you need to talk or just need company."	*"Others have it worse than you; you shouldn't feel so sad."*
"It's okay to feel sad. Do you want to share why you're feeling this way?"	Telling them to smile more and that it's all in their head.
Offer a comforting presence, giving them the opportunity to talk or be together is silence.	Forcing them to engage in activities they're not up for, to "cheer them up."

Grief is a
testament to
our capacity for
love,
showcasing the
depth and
meaning of our
connections
that have been
lost.

GRIEF

Meet Your Grief

Grief is a profound emotional response that arises when we experience the loss of something irreplaceable. This could be a person, a significant place, or a cherished stage of life. Engaging with grief allows us to fully confront and honor the importance of our loss, reflecting deeply on the impact of what we've had to let go.

Detailed Explanation of Grief

Grief challenges us to face the reality of a permanent absence, pushing us to adapt to a life without something or someone we deeply valued. Grief arises when we face the loss of something deeply important to us, a loss that is final and beyond our control. This sets grief apart from sadness, which is often tied to hopes or desires that haven't been met yet but still might be. Grief requires us to accept that something we valued is permanently gone, prompting us to find a way to live with this new reality.

By working through grief, we learn to honor what we've lost, reflect on its importance, and eventually find a way to move forward while keeping the memory of the loss as a part of who we are.

Advice from Grief

If grief could give you some friendly advice, it would likely say:

- *"Seek out supportive relationships that can provide comfort and understanding as you navigate through your loss."*

- *"Find meaningful ways to memorialize the lost, ensuring that your journey through grief is transformative and not a stagnant endpoint."*

- *"Embrace the full intensity of your grief as a reflection of your deep love and the value of your lost connection."*

Mood-State Grief

Emotions are meant to be fleeting, prompting necessary actions and resolving as those actions are taken. Although the intensity may decrease over time, grief frequently comes and goes for a very long time. Sometimes, it lasts forever. However, if grief is not adequately addressed, it can evolve into a more persistent state, characterized by:

- **Persistent Sorrow:** A deep, enduring anguish that lingers long, long after the loss.

- **Detachment:** A withdrawal from life's engagements, often feeling numb or disconnected.

- **Preoccupation with the Lost:** Continual rumination on the person or thing that was lost, impacting daily functioning.

GRIEF

Coping Skills for Grief

All emotions arise with varying levels of intensity. When navigating intense grief, these skills can empower you to engage more effectively:

- **Support Groups:** Participate in groups where you can share and process your grief with others who understand.

- **Memorial Activities:** Create personal rituals or memorials that help you remember and honor your lost loved one.

- **Professional Counseling:** Consider engaging with a therapist who specializes in grief to guide you through your new life without your loved one.

Repressing, Reacting, & Engaging with Grief

Your response to grief can significantly influence your health and wellbeing. Let's say you've lost a loved one...

Repress	**React**	**Engage**
Acting as if life is unchanged, avoiding acknowledgment of the loss.	Becoming overwhelmed by grief to the extent that daily life becomes unmanageable.	Actively seeking support, whether through friends, family, or professionals, and finding constructive ways to process and honor your loss.

Positive Outcomes When You Engage with Grief:

- **Healing:** Fully experiencing and expressing grief can facilitate a process of emotional healing, enabling you to adapt to the loss.

- **Personal Growth:** Grief can lead to significant personal insights, fostering resilience and a deeper appreciation for life.

- **Strengthened Bonds:** Sharing your grief can deepen relationships with others who have faced similar losses or who can empathize with your experience, offering mutual support and understanding.

Ideas for Supporting Someone Else's Grief

Emotionally Intelligent Options	**Not so Emotionally Intelligent Options**
- *"I'm so sorry for your loss. I'm willing to listen if you'd like to talk and I'm also happy to sit quietly with you."* - *"Would you like to share any fond memories you have?"* - Respect their process and offer practical support, such as helping with daily tasks.	- *"It's been a while now; you should be moving on."* - Comparing their loss to someone else's to minimize their feelings. - Avoiding discussions about their loss because it makes you uncomfortable.

Shame can be a very uncomfortable yet powerful invitation to confront and heal our deepest wounds.

SHAME

Meet Your Shame

Shame is the emotion that arises when our relationship with ourselves is compromised. Perhaps the most difficult of all emotions, shame indicates the need to reevaluate, mend and strengthen our self-identity. Shame relates to how we feel about ourselves as a whole—it's an internal sense of being fundamentally flawed or unworthy.

Detailed Explanation of Shame

An irreducible need of all men, women, and children is a sense of connection and belonging. Shame arises when the way we feel about ourselves as a whole is fundamentally flawed, reprehensible and unworthy of this connection. Although shame may be tied to a specific incident, it reflects back on a person's entire identity.

Shame and guilt are often mistaken for one another. While shame is about self-identity (I am bad) guilt, on the other hand, is typically about a specific behavior or action (I did something bad).

Advice from Shame

If shame could give you some friendly advice, it would likely say:

- *"Seek out compassion and understanding, both from yourself and from others, to help re-build connection and belonging."*

- *"Use me as a springboard for personal growth and self-acceptance, rather than a reason for isolation or self-rejection."*

- *"Challenge the beliefs that fuel me. Recognize that you are more than your mistakes or how others may judge you."*

Mood-State Shame

Emotions are meant to be temporary, prompting action and resolving once that action is taken. However, if not properly addressed, shame can evolve into a persistent mood state, characterized by:

- **Self-Loathing:** Persistent feelings of being unworthy or fundamentally flawed.

- **Social Anxiety:** Intense anxiety in social settings due to a fear of judgment or rejection.

- **Isolation:** Withdrawal from social interactions to avoid feelings of shame.

"Challenge the beliefs that fuel me. Recognize that you are more than your mistakes or how others may judge you."

SHAME

Coping Skills for Shame

All emotions arise with varying levels of intensity. When navigating intense shame, these skills can empower you to engage more effectively:

- **Positive Affirmations:** Regularly engage in affirmations that reinforce your inherent worth and challenge the basis of your shame.

- **Sharing Your Feelings:** Discuss your experiences of shame in a supportive environment, as expressing these feelings can help diminish their intensity.

- **Cognitive-Behavioral Techniques:** Actively challenge and reframe negative thoughts that perpetuate shame, promoting a healthier self-image.

Repressing, Reacting, & Engaging with Shame

Your response to shame can significantly influence your self-esteem, confidence and self-worth. Let's say your significant other has broken off your relationship...

Repress	React	Engage
Ignoring feelings of unworthiness or pretending they don't exist.	Lashing out at others with insensitive and unkind remarks in an effort to redirect your pain elsewhere.	Acknowledging and exploring the root cause for your shame, thinking objectively and seeking out supportive dialogues to challenge and transform negative self-beliefs.

Positive Outcomes When You Engage with Shame:

- **Self-Acceptance:** Directly confronting shame can foster deeper self-acceptance and diminish self-criticism.

- **Breaking Cycles:** Understanding and processing shame can interrupt negative behavioral patterns, leading to healthier habits and relationships.

- **Enhanced Authenticity:** Working through shame encourages a more authentic life, embracing both your strengths and vulnerabilities.

Ideas for Supporting Someone Else's Shame

Emotionally Intelligent Options	Not so Emotionally Intelligent Options
"It sounds like you're being really hard on yourself. Everyone has moments they're not proud of."	*"Well, if I were you, I'd be ashamed too."*
"You're not alone. If you want to talk about it, I'm here to listen without judgment."	Highlighting how they always seem to mess up without offering any empathy or support.
Encourage them to share their feelings and reassure them of their worth and the possibility of moving forward.	Making the conversation about your discomfort with their shame rather than their feelings.

Next Steps

Part Three: Next Steps

There is an emotion behind every action we take. Learning to work with our emotions, rather than working against them dramatically improves the quality of one's life. It leads to stronger interpersonal relationships, better conflict resolution, effective problem solving, improved health and wellness and even financial stability! It would be very tough, more like impossible, to come up with anything that isn't impacted by the way we respond to our emotions!

Unfortunately, we are bombarded with messages throughout our Western civilization that encourage us to deny and avoid our "negative" emotions. Hopefully by now, you are starting to see how there are no negative emotions. Yes, some emotions are more difficult to experience than others, but an emotion in and of itself, is not what's negative. Our thoughts that cause the emotions to arise, and how we respond to emotions can be negative but it's time to stop blaming emotions.

You've made it to this last chapter, and that's a great sign! So, what's next?

Emotional Literacy

A good place to start is building a strong foundation of Emotional Literacy. Although this book is a great starting point for understanding several specific emotions, there's a lot more to emotions than that! For example, did you know there is a difference between *emotion energy* and *emotion intensity*? And did you know emotions are not mutually exclusive and that several emotions can arise at the same time?

Building a strong foundation of Emotional Literacy is like learning how to operate a car. Once you understand the basics, it opens the door to a whole new world of opportunities!

Recommended Reading
If you're interested in dipping your toe into the Emotional Literacy pool, I recommend reading the following two books. These are both great reads written by two thought leaders who are well-versed in emotions!

- ***Atlas of the Heart*** written by Brene Brown, PhD, MSW

- ***Emotional Agility*** written by Susan David, PhD

If you've already read these books and are interested in reading more, some of the other books I recommend include:

- **_The Language of Emotions_** written by Karla McLaren M.Ed.

- **_Mindset_** written by Carol S. Dweck, PhD

- **_How Emotions are Made_** written by Lisa Feldman Barrett, PhD

- **_Go Suck a Lemon_** written by Michael Cornwall PsyD, Ph.D.

- **_The Happiness Hypothesis_** written by Jonathan Haidt

- **_Thinking, Fast and Slow_** written by Daniel Kahneman, PhD

- **_Permission to Feel_** written by Marc Brackett, PhD

- **_Personality isn't Permanent_** written by Benjamin Hardy, PhD

- **_The Upside of Your Dark Side_** written by Todd Kashdan, PhD, Robert Biswas-Diener, and Dr. Philos

Digital Course
Emotional Literacy is the ability to recognize, understand, and name one's own emotions and the emotions of others. It's akin to learning the alphabet before being able to read and write; it's the foundational knowledge of emotions.

If you're looking for a high-impact, interactive, online learning experience, I strongly recommend the Emotional Literacy course I've developed!

Without the ability to understand and identify emotions, it's challenging (maybe even impossible) to manage them effectively or use them in ways that lead to positive outcomes.

This comprehensive, self-paced, digital course covers a variety of topics including:

- **The Emotion Flow** – A step-by-step flowchart depicting when and why emotions activate and your options for responding.
- **Four Emotion Categories** – A simplified way of logically organizing all emotions
- **Emotion Intensity vs Emotion Energy** – An often overlooked distinction that can be especially helpful with identifying emotions in complex situations.
- **Emotions are Always True but They aren't Always Right** – A key concept for anyone interested in becoming more nimble when navigating emotions.
- **Feelings vs Emotions** – Another practical tip for identifying emotions in complex situations.
- **Emotions Synonyms List** – Over 200 words used to describe 11 basic emotions.
- **Emotions are Not Mutually Exclusive** – What's really happening when more than one emotion is active at the same time? (Spoiler Alert: This happens most of the time.)
- And so much more…!

Remember, without a solid foundation of Emotional Literacy, you can't be Emotionally Intelligent. For more information on this digital course, please visit EmotionalLiteracy.com.

Emotional Intelligence

Perhaps you're familiar with the phrase "A person is ready when they are ready." Learning how to leverage your emotions to strengthen your relationships, health and wellness, and even your financial stability can be a life-changing experience. If you're a person who is excited and ready for an immersive learning experience, I've got the program for you!

Empowered by Emotions Program
I offer a comprehensive signature program called Empowered by Emotions. It starts off with Emotional Literacy and moves right into Emotional Intelligence. It's everything you need, nuts to bolts for tapping into your emotional superpowers!

Emotional Intelligence builds on the foundation of Emotional Literacy. It involves the knowledge and skills to manage one's own emotions effectively, navigate emotional situations, make decisions based on information derived from your emotions, and influence or help regulate the emotions of others.

The focus of Emotional Intelligence is taking things to the next level. It's all about the application of understanding emotions. It's about using the knowledge of emotions gained from Emotional Literacy to engage in self-regulation, self-discipline, empathy, motivation, and strengthening social skills.

Emotional Intelligence is essential for optimizing personal well-being, successful relationships, and goal achievement. It allows individuals to navigate the complexities of social interactions and personal challenges with a level of finesse and understanding that leads to more positive outcomes!

At the time this book is being written, the Empowered by Emotions program is offered publicly twice a year in March and September. It is also available via an exclusive 1:1 delivery model.

For more information, please visit EmpoweredByEmotions.com/SignatureProgram.

Conclusion

Thank you for taking the time to become more informed about your emotions! Remember, the insights and skills you've gained are tools that can transform not just your own life, but also the lives of those around you.

As you set forth and apply what you've learned, expect to see positive changes in how you relate to yourself and others. You're not just reacting to life anymore; you're actively shaping your experiences with wisdom and insights from your emotions. Keep nurturing your emotional skills, and you'll find that you're able to face challenges with greater resilience and seize opportunities with enhanced enthusiasm.

This isn't the end of your learning path—it's just the beginning. Each day offers new chances to practice and deepen your emotional intelligence. Stay curious, remain open, and be willing to explore the nuances of your emotions. As you do, you'll discover that every emotion, whether joyous or challenging, is a guidepost on your path to a fulfilled and balanced life.

Thank you for allowing me to be a part of your journey. I'm excited to see where your newfound knowledge takes you. Keep moving forward, keep learning, and remember: the world of emotions is as rich and boundless as the universe itself, with limitless potential for growth and transformation.

Working with your emotions rather than working against them empowers you at every step!

Go to EmpoweredByEmotions.com to download resources, place bulk orders, book Lisa C. Welsher for keynote speeches, and to learn more about the Empowered by Emotions training programs.

Want to buy a lot of these books? Fantastic! We need more people in the world who are informed about their emotions and I can help!

Please contact me at lisa.welsher@empoweredbyemotions.com for more information.

About Lisa

Emotional Intelligence has literally transformed my life. My own experiences with challenging relationships, conflict, stress, and overwhelming responsibilities have deeply informed my approach to emotional wellness and resilience.

All things related to emotions have always interested me, evolving over three decades from a personal curiosity into a life's mission. What began as a quest for understanding has blossomed into a dedication to empowering people with the superpower that comes from working with your emotions rather than working against them.

Becoming more informed about emotions has been a game-changer in every facet of my life, particularly in strengthening my relationships, enhancing my health and wellness, and even bolstering my financial stability.

My "first mountain" was a rewarding 25-year career in management consulting, where I navigated the complex dynamics of the corporate world. Throughout this time, I witnessed firsthand how emotions such as anger, anxiety, guilt, fear, and shame frequently became the undercurrent of inefficiencies, leading to significant time and energy wasted in the workplace.

These weren't just fleeting moments; they were powerful forces, often the root cause behind vast amounts of wasted time and energy, not only in the workplace but spilling over into home life as well. The ripple effects of these emotional undercurrents on teamwork, productivity, and personal well-being highlighted the critical need for emotional literacy and intelligence in fostering healthier, more effective environments both professionally and personally.

Focused now on my "second mountain," I have the good fortune of being able to pivot my attention. I am now dedicated full-time to empowering individuals with the tools of emotional literacy and emotional intelligence. This transition marks not just a change in my career path but a deeper commitment to paving the way for profound transformations in people's lives.

I can't say I ever wanted to be a DJ, but now I sort of am...
Just like a great DJ who becomes very knowledgeable about different artists and different songs, I've become very knowledgeable about the various thought leaders in the space of emotional literacy and emotional intelligence, which includes all sorts of concepts, principles, and skills.

And... just like it's the DJ's responsibility to put together an exceptional playlist to rock the house... I see it as my responsibility to put together exceptional "playlists" of emotional literacy and emotional intelligence greatest hits.

I am not a therapist, researcher, or clinical scientist. I am an educator. By embracing emotions, I've learned the art of communication that deepens connections, resolves conflicts with compassion, and builds trust and understanding in ways I never thought possible.

This work has not only brought me closer to my loved ones but has also significantly reduced stress and anxiety, leading to a profound improvement in my overall health and well-being. Financially, being in tune with my emotions has empowered me to make more thoughtful decisions, manage stress around money more effectively, and approach my career and financial opportunities with confidence and clarity.

This holistic enhancement of my life is a testament to the power of aligning with our emotions, and it's a gift I am passionate about sharing with others.

To learn more about my current work and offerings, please visit EmpoweredByEmotions.com or follow Empowered by Emotions on the various social media platforms.